SHADOW AND SUBSTANCE

SHADOW AND SUBSTANCE

TAOIST MYSTICAL REFLECTIONS

edited and with photographs by
CATHARINE HUGHES

A CROSSROAD BOOK
THE SEABURY PRESS • NEW YORK

Designed by Joseph Vesely

Copyright © 1974 by the Seabury Press, Inc.

Library of Congress Cataloging in Publication Data

Hughes, Catharine   comp.
    Shadow and substance: Taoist mystical reflections.

   "A Crossroad book."
   1. Taoism—Collected works.   I. Title.
BL1900.A1H8   181'.09'514   74-12189
ISBN 0-8164-2104-8

Manufactured in the United States of America

The wisdom and mysticism of the East have very much to give us even though they speak their own language which it is impossible to imitate. They should remind us of that which is familiar in our own culture and which we have already forgotten, and we should direct our attention to that which we have put aside as insignificant, namely the fate of our own inner man.

—Carl G. Jung

ACKNOWLEDGMENTS

The Canon of Reason and Virtue, by Lao Tzu, translated by D. T. Suzuki and Paul Carus. Open Court Publishing Company, 1913.

The Secret and Sublime: Taoist Mysteries and Magic, by John Blofeld. Copyright © 1973 by George Allen and Unwin Ltd.

The Tai Shang Tractate and the Writings of Chuang Tzu (Part II), translated by James Legge. Oxford University Press, 1891.

The Tao Te Ching of Lao Tzu and the Writings of Chuang Tzu (Part I), translated by James Legge. Oxford University Press, 1891.

The Way of Life: Tao Te Ching, by Lao Tzu, translated by R. B. Blakney. Copyright © 1955 by Raymond B. Blakney. Reprinted by permission of the New American Library of World Literature, Inc.

INTRODUCTION

Although it is impossible to determine with accuracy precisely when Taoism was founded, historians generally credit Lao Tzu, who was born in approximately 570 B.C., and to whom is ascribed the classic of Taoist mysticism, the *Tao Te Ching* (literally, "The Book of the Way and Its [Hidden] Power").

The word "Tao" itself means "way," "road," or "path," a way both transcendent and immanent, ultimate and nameless Reality. Or, as is said in the *Tao Te Ching:*

Like the gods of the shrine in the home,
    So The Way and its mystery waits
In the world of material things:
    The good man's treasure,
The bad man's refuge.

Many of the poems and reflections in the *Tao Te Ching* are practical rather than mystical, providing moral and even political advice, which is hardly surprising in a century that also produced Kung Tzu (Confucius). But

INTRODUCTION

where they *are* mystical, they have much in common with the mysticism of other periods, religions, and cultures. As R. B. Blakney observes in his *Lao Tzu,* "The Chinese mystics were original and to the point in their writings, but their point was identical with that of the great mystics elsewhere."

Lao Tzu was suspicious of systems, whether political or ethical, as "artificial" and likely to pervert man's innate simplicity. He held that they led him toward aggressive, self-centered behavior, made him competitive, and ultimately gave him delusions about himself. From this sprang hatred and schism, wars and the potential destruction of society. To counter this, he proposed as the ideal a small primitive community made up of villages in which men would live in harmony with The Way:

It was when the Great Tao declined
That there appeared humanity and
     righteousness.
It was when knowledge and intelligence
     arose
That there appeared much hypocrisy.

Although it may at first glance seem excessively subtle to the Westerner—almost scornful of the idea of "humanity"—what Lao Tzu actually seems to be suggesting is that, as the late Thomas Merton wrote in *Mystics and Zen Masters,*

> the *reality* of humanity and righteousness is right there in front of your nose if only you will practice them without self-conscious reflection, or self-congratulation, and without trying to explain and justify your acts by ethical theory. . . . As soon as man becomes aware of doing good and avoiding evil, he is no longer perfectly good.

What, then, is The Way? Initially, it is a void, never filled, but out of which all things issue. In other words, the source of the world (which corresponds to the Hindu concept of Brahman). "A deep pool it is, never to run dry." In the *Tao Te Ching* it is described as even "prior to God."

The difficulties in conveying the essence of Taoism are suggested by Lao Tzu's own words: "He who knows does not speak." Personal intuition is central to it, but, despite his reluctance to rely on the word, Lao Tzu did apparently write a five thousand-word treatise and his disciples were later to record his thoughts—whether altogether accurately it is impossible to know—in more detail; unbroken silence clearly was not sufficient, one had to write and speak even about the ineffable.

Taoist mysticism insists that the thinker and the thought, the one who beholds and that which is beheld, are one. It requires that one renounce knowledge, logic, reason, and analysis in favor of perfect stillness, both internal and external, and permit the mind to penetrate all objects, with self-consciousness eliminated. Only in that way can one be liberated; only in that way can there be complete harmony.

In *The Secret and Sublime,* John Blofeld recounts what he heard from an ancient Taoist:

> The Tao is to be found in inner stillness. It reveals itself as One—timeless, formless, all-pervading. In it all creatures and objects have their being. . . . Apart from the totality which is the Tao, they have no being. The Tao and the myriad objects *are not two!* Unlike water which rises from the lake as vapor and flows back to it in streams, the Tao's creations do not rise from it, nor do they return to it, they and the Tao having never at any time been apart. They *are* the Tao. This faculty of

being one and many simultaneously is a mystery that can be apprehended but not explained.

And this, obscure though it initially may seem, really is the essence of Taoism. When John C. H. Wu translated the Gospel of St. John into Chinese some forty years ago, he began: "In the beginning was Tao, and Tao was with God, and Tao was God."

But, again, what *is* the Tao? On the one hand it is poetic—great poetry—at least as embodied in the *Tao Te Ching*. And to Westerners it sometimes seems at least a little quaint. Yet, it also frequently recalls the Sermon on the Mount.

The word "Ching" has had many translations. It is a "classic," a "book," but also something appreciably more. For Taoism it is the equivalent of the Bible. It is authoritative, provides the core, the essence, the reality, of Taoism. But, as Merton wrote, if there is a correct answer to the question: "What is the Tao?" it is "I don't know."

"The whole secret of life lies in the discovery of this Tao, which can never be discovered," says Merton. And the quest is not simply intellectual; one must alter every aspect of his being, must achieve something that involves both perfect activity and perfect rest. He must possess a view and an attitude toward the world that sees it as something not to be tampered with, not to be spoiled. He must enter into communion with it.

Dwight Goddard has written that Tao is "the name given to perhaps the grandest conception the human mind has ever conceived." In his introduction to *Taoist Tales,* Raymond Van Over contends that

> to understand the Tao one must first realize that the heavenly Tao simply pursues its course and does not speak about it or symbolize its essence. . . . If resistance is met, it is best to rest passively until it is exhausted and then go on one's way. . . . Another, perhaps more popular analogy sees man as the "thinking reed," who moves with the wind and is not broken as a rigid stalk would be.

Confucius, who as has been noted was a man of the same century as Lao Tzu, sought a government position in order to effect his ideas. Lao Tzu went his own way. He did, however, have successors, men like Li Po, who many regard as China's greatest poet, who, Van Over writes, "was often drunk with rice wine as well as the Tao." As a young man,

INTRODUCTION

Li Po enjoyed sword fighting and the martial arts and, according to legend, met his death—while drunk—as he attempted to embrace a reflection in the water. Thence to be carried off by a dolphin. Whether drunk, whether carried off by a dolphin, or not, his poetry is that of a committed and ardent Taoist:

Gladly we say: "Here is a place to rest."
The goodly wine in waving circles goes.
Our souls extoll the sweet fir-laden air,
Till ere we cease each star but dimly glows.

Drunken am I—and you with pleasure too—
In pure enjoyment, free from human woes.

Or, perhaps more seriously:

The living is a passing traveler;
The dead a man come home.
One brief journey betwixt heaven and earth,
Then, alas! we are the same old dust of
    ten thousand ages. . . .
Man dies, his white bones are dumb without
    a word
When the green pines feel the coming of
    the spring.

Taoism is, of course, a nonconforming, even an iconoclastic, religion, providing what

INTRODUCTION

D. T. Suzuki calls "a most eloquent protest, when you have the eye to see, against the baneful influence of modern culture." It insists—and Chuang Tzu in particular insisted—that men should not acquiesce in any role that reduces their individuality; that they should return to a simpler life, a life closer to nature. It is, in all probability, predominantly this quality that accounts for the renewed interest in Taoism in the West, where an increasingly technological society tends to suppress rather than reinforce the person, the in-the-end necessarily private being, faced with necessarily personal, private, moments of truth and decision.

SHADOW AND SUBSTANCE

The secret waits for the insight
  Of eyes unclouded by longing;
Those who are bound by desire
  See only the outward container.
          —Lao Tzu

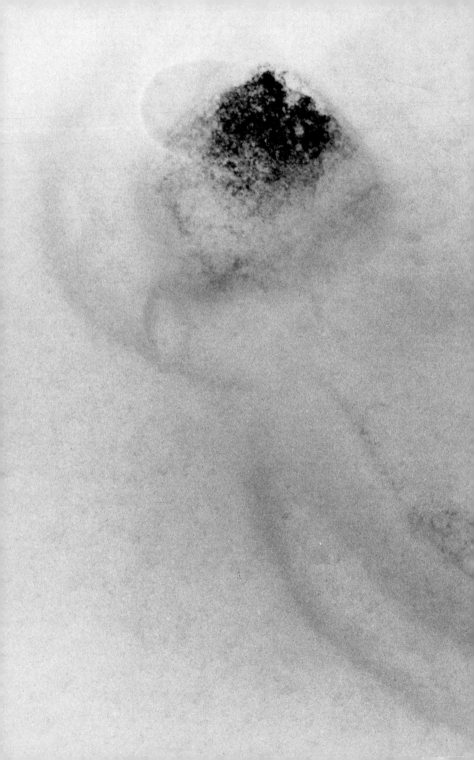

Like the gods of the shrine in the home,
   So The Way and its mystery waits
In the world of material things:
   The good man's treasure,
The bad man's refuge.
   Fair wordage is ever for sale;
Fair manners are worn like a cloak;
   But why should there be such a waste
Of the badness in men?
   How used the ancients to honor The Way?
Didn't they say that the seeker may find it,
   And that sinners who find are forgiven?
So did they lift up The Way and its Virtue
   Above everything else in the world.
                                    —Lao Tzu

Man at his birth is supple and weak; at his death, firm and strong. So it is with all things. Trees and plants, in their early growth, are soft and brittle; at their death, dry and withered.

Thus it is that firmness and strength are the concomitants of death; softness and weakness, the concomitants of life.

Hence he who relies on the strength of his forces does not conquer; and a tree which is strong will fill the outstretched arms, [and thereby invites the feller].

Therefore the place of what is firm and strong is below, and that of what is soft and weak is above.

—Lao Tzu

How do I know that the love of life is not a delusion and that the dislike of death is not like a young person's losing his way, and not knowing that he is [really] going home? . . . How do I know that the dead do not repent of their former craving for life?
                              —Chuang Tzu

Or fame or life,
    Which do you hold more dear?
Or life or wealth,
    To which would you adhere?
Keep life and lose those other things;
Keep them and lose your life—which
        brings
        Sorrow and pain more near?

Thus we may see,
    Who cleaves to fame
    Rejects what is more great;
Who loves large stores
    Gives up the richer state.

Who is content
Needs fear no shame.
Who knows to stop
Incurs no blame.
From danger free
Long live shall he.

                            —Lao Tzu

Thirty spokes will converge
In the hub of a wheel;
But the use of the cart
Will depend on the part
Of the hub that is void.

With a wall all around
A clay bowl is molded;
But the use of the bowl
Will depend on the part
Of the bowl that is void.

Cut out windows and doors
In the house as you build;
But the use of the house
Will depend on the space
In the walls that is void.

So advantage is had
From whatever is there;
But usefulness rises
From what is not.

—Lao Tzu

Each season has its ending and beginning; each age has its changes and transformations; misery and happiness regularly alternate. Here our views are thwarted, and yet the result may afterwards have our approval; there we insist on our own views, and looking at things differently from others, try to correct them, while we are in error ourselves.

—Chuang Tzu

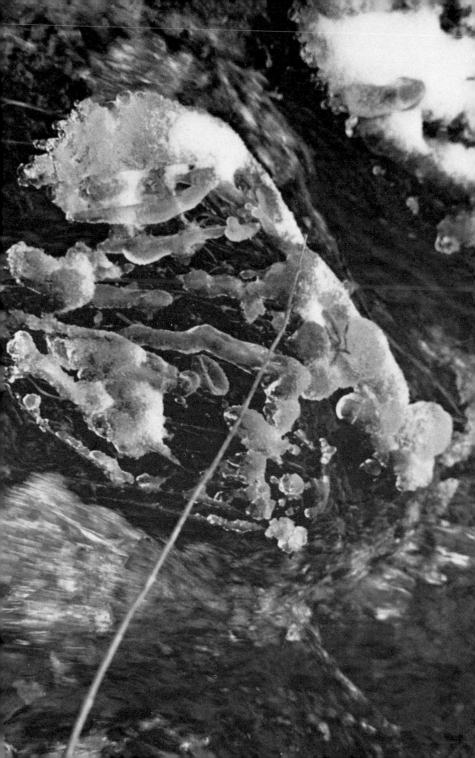

If one observes the Way of Heaven
and maintains Its doings [as his own]
all that he has to do is accomplished.
　　　　　　—Yin Fu Ching

Something there is, whose veiled creation was
Before the earth or sky began to be;
So silent, so aloof and so alone,
It changes not, nor fails, but touches all:
Conceive it as the mother of the world.

I do not know its name;
A name for it is "Way";
Pressed for designation,
I call it Great.
Great means outgoing,
Outgoing, far-reaching,
Far-reaching, return.

The Way is great,
The sky is great,
The earth is great,
The king also is great.
Within the realm
These four are great;
The king but stands
For one of them.

Man conforms to the earth;
The earth conforms to the sky;
The sky conforms to the Way;
The Way conforms to its own nature.

—Lao Tzu

Abstaining from speech marks him who is obeying the spontaneity of his nature. A violent wind does not last for a whole morning; a sudden rain does not last for the whole day. To whom is it that these [two] things are owing? To Heaven and Earth. If Heaven and Earth cannot make such actings last long, how much less can man!

—Lao Tzu

Who knows his manhood's strength,
Yet still his female feebleness maintains;
As to one channel flow the many drains,
All come to him, yea, all beneath the sky.
Thus he the constant excellence retains—
The simple child again, free from all stains.

Who knows how white attracts,
Yet always keeps himself within black's shade,
The pattern of humility displayed,
Displayed in view of all beneath the sky;
He in the unchanging excellence arrayed,
Endless return to man's first state has made.

Who knows how glory shines,
Yet loves disgrace, nor e'er for it is pale;
Behold his presence in a spacious vale,
To which men come from all beneath the sky.
The unchanging excellence completes its tale;
The simple infant man in him we hail.

—Lao Tzu

Hatred and kindness; taking and giving; re-proof and instruction; death and life—these eight things are instruments of rectification, but only those are able to use them who do not obstinately refuse to comply with their great changes. Hence it is said, "Correction is rectification." When the minds of some do not acknowledge this, it is because the gate of Heaven [in them] has not been opened.

—Chuang Tzu

Those who think that wealth is the proper thing for them cannot give up their revenues; those who seek distinction cannot give up the thought of fame; those who cleave to power cannot give the handle of it to others. While they hold their grasp of those things, they are afraid of losing them. When they let them go, they are grieved and they will not look at a single example, from which they might perceive the folly of their restless pursuits—such men are under the doom of Heaven.

—Chuang Tzu

It is wisdom to know others;
  It is enlightenment to know one's self.
                              —Lao Tzu

Gentleness is sure to be victorious even in battle and firmly to maintain its ground. Heaven will save its possessor, by his [very] gentleness protecting him.

—Lao Tzu

There are no special doors for calamity and happiness; they come as men themselves call them. Their recompenses follow good and evil as the shadow follows the substance.
—The Thai-Shang

In the Way of Heaven, there is no partiality of love; it is always on the side of the good man.

—Lao Tzu

There are ways but the Way is
    uncharted;
There are names but not nature
    in words:
Nameless indeed is the source
    of creation
But things have a mother and she
    has a name.

—Lao Tzu

Simplicity without a name
Is free from all external aim.
With no desire, at rest and still,
All things go right as of their will.

—Lao Tzu

There is the vulgar saying, "The multitude of men consider gain to be the most important thing; pure scholars, fame; those who are wise and able value their ambition; the sage prizes essential purity." Therefore simplicity is the denomination of that in which there is no admixture; purity of that in which the spirit is not impaired. It is he who can embody simplicity and purity whom we call the True Man

—Chuang Tzu

It is not enough for you to suppose that you know these things. You must perceive them directly. Listening to sermons, memorizing classics, will do you no good. You must look within your mind. Even then you will see nothing clearly, unless you lose awareness of a self that looks. There is no such person, I assure you—there is a looking, but no looker. Yet banishing the concept of being one who looks can be difficult. Therefore prepare yourself by limiting your desires, requiring nothing of the world beyond what is needed for sustaining bodily well-being. Meanwhile, practice the art of *kuan* [inner vision] daily. This will still the restless waves of thought and sharpen your awareness. Awareness must be acute, but objectless. No looker, no looked-at, just looking. Do you understand? I mean your mind must be indifferent to the objects it reflects, performing its function like a mirror. When there is no attachment, true seeing arises. With seeing comes serenity. Serenity puts an end to woe. In the absence of woe, joy will fill your body to overflowing. Certainty of the rightness of your doing and of the truth of your seeing will flush your cheeks and make your eyebrows dance.

—Anon.

The straight tree is the first to be cut down; the well of sweet water is the first to be exhausted. Your aim is to embellish your wisdom so as to startle the ignorant and to cultivate your person to show the unsightliness of others. A light shines around you as if you were carrying with you the sun and moon, and thus it is that you do not escape such calamity. Formerly I heard a highly accomplished man say, "Those who boast have no merit. The merit which is deemed complete will begin to wane." Who can rid himself of [the ideas of] merit and fame, and return and put himself on the level of the masses of men? The practice of the Tao flows abroad, but its master does not care to dwell where it can be seen; his attainments in it hold their course, but he does not wish to appear in its display. Always simple and commonplace, he may seem to be bereft of reason. He obliterates the traces of his action, gives up position and power, and aims not at merit and fame. Therefore he does not censure men and men do not censure him. The perfect man does not seek to be heard of; how is it that you delight in doing so?

—Chuang Tzu

Heaven is long-enduring and earth continues long. The reason why heaven and earth are able to endure and continue thus long is because they do not live of, or for, themselves. This is how they are able to continue and endure. Therefore the sage puts his own person last, and yet it is found in the foremost place; he treats his person as if it were foreign to him, and yet that person is preserved. Is it not because he has no personal and private ends that therefore such ends are realized?
—Lao Tzu

The world may be known
  Without leaving the house;
The Way may be seen
  Apart from the windows.
The further you go,
  The less you will know.
Accordingly, the wise man
  Knows without going,
Sees without seeing,
  Does without doing.

—Lao Tzu

That whereby the rivers and seas are able to receive the homage and tribute of all the valley streams is their skill in being lower than they; it is thus that they are the kings of them all. So it is that the sage [ruler], wishing to be above men, puts himself by his words below them, and, wishing to be before them, places his person behind them.

In this way, though he has his place above them, men do not feel his weight, nor though he has his place before them, do they feel it an injury to them.

Therefore all in the world delight to exalt him and do not weary of him. Because he does not strive, no one finds it possible to strive with him.

—Lao Tzu

You have heard of flying with wings, but never of flying without wings. You have heard of the knowledge that knows, but never of the knowledge that does not know. Look into the closed room, the empty chamber where brightness is born! Fortune and blessing gather where there is stillness. But if you do not keep still— this is called sitting but racing around. Let your ears and eyes communicate with what is inside, and put mind and knowledge on the outside. . . . Can you really make your body like a withered tree, your mind like dead ashes?

—Chuang Tzu

Let desire be stilled while you contemplate the Mystery; when desires reign, you behold only its outward manifestations.

—Lao Tzu

When the people do not fear what they ought to fear, that which is their great dread will come to them.

Let them not thoughtlessly indulge themselves in their ordinary life; let them not act as if weary of what that life depends on.

It is by avoiding such indulgence that such weariness does not arise.

—Lao Tzu

He who knows other men is discerning; he who knows himself is intelligent. He who overcomes others is strong; he who overcomes himself is mighty. He who is satisfied with his lot is rich; he who goes on acting with energy has a firm will. He who does not fail in the requirements of his position, continues long; he who dies and yet does not perish, has longevity.

—Lao Tzu

Among the dead there are no rulers above, no subjects below, and no chores of the four seasons.

—Chuang Tzu

When I speak of goodness and of beauty, I speak of the Tao. When I speak of bad and ugly, I speak of the Tao. Self is the Tao. Other is the Tao. Distinctions between opposites are false at the beginning, illusory in the middle, and erroneous at the end. If you suppose otherwise, you will be tormented by demons— demon longings, demon fears. You will struggle all your life against fiends of your own imagining, weighing gain against loss as though there could be anything in the entire universe that is not yours already. What wasted energy! What needless tears!

—Anon.

The partial becomes complete; the crooked, straight; the empty, full; the worn out, new. He whose desires are few gets them; he whose desires are many goes astray.

—Lao Tzu

The tree which fills the arms grew from the tiniest sprout; the tower of nine storeys rose from a small heap of earth; the journey of a thousand li commenced with a single step.
—Lao Tzu

There is no end or beginning to the Tao. Things indeed die and are born, not reaching a perfect state which can be relied on. Now there is emptiness, and now fulness—they do not continue in one form. The years cannot be reproduced; time cannot be arrested. Decay and growth, fulness and emptiness, when they end, begin again. It is thus that we describe the method of great righteousness and discourse about the principle pervading all things. The life of things is like the hurrying and galloping along of a horse. With every movement there is a change; with every moment there is an alteration. What should you be doing? What should you not be doing? You have only to be allowing this course of natural transformation to be going on.

—Chuang Tzu

When a man knows what is not useful, you can then begin to speak to him of what is useful. The earth for instance is certainly spacious and great; but what a man uses of it is only sufficient ground for his feet. If, however, a rent were made by the side of his feet, down to the yellow springs, could the man still make use of it? Hui Tzu said, "He could not use it," and Chuang Tzu rejoined, "Then the usefulness of what is of no use is clear."

—Chuang Tzu

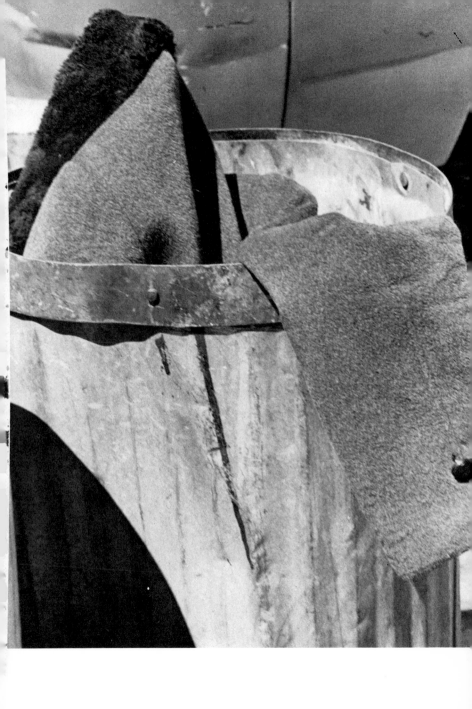

The perception of what is small is [the secret of] clear-sightedness; the guarding of what is soft and tender is [the secret of] strength.

—Lao Tzu

To regard benevolence as the source of all kindness, righteousness as the source of all distinctions, propriety as the rule of all conduct, and music as the idea of all harmony, thus diffusing a fragrance of gentleness and goodness, constitutes what we call the superior man.

—Chuang Tzu

In the highest antiquity, [the people] did not know that there were [their rulers]. In the next age they loved them and praised them. In the next they feared them. In the next they despised them. Thus it was that when faith [in the Tao] was deficient [in the rulers] a want of faith in them ensued [in the people].

—Lao Tzu

To rejoice over a victory is to rejoice over
    the slaughter of men!
Hence a man who rejoices over the slaughter
    of men cannot expect to thrive in the
      world of men.
. . . Every victory is a funeral.

—Lao Tzu

Misery! Happiness is to be found by its side! Happiness! Misery lurks beneath it! Who knows what either will come to in the end?

—Lao Tzu

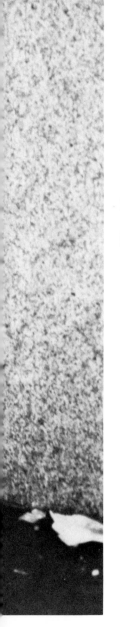

Because I am merciful, therefore
    I can be brave . . .
For heaven will come to the rescue
    of the merciful and protect him
      with *its* mercy.

                      —Lao Tzu

The reason why all men do not obtain the True Tao is because their minds are perverted. Their minds being perverted, their spirits become perturbed. Their minds being perturbed, they are attracted towards external things. Being attracted towards external things, they begin to seek for them greedily. This greedy quest leads to perplexities and annoyances; and these again result in disordered thoughts, which cause anxiety and trouble to both body and mind. The parties then meet with foul disgraces, flow wildly on through the phases of life and death, are liable constantly to sink in the sea of bitterness, and forever lose the True Tao.

—The Thai-Shang

That which kills life does not die; that
which gives life does not live.
—Chuang Tzu

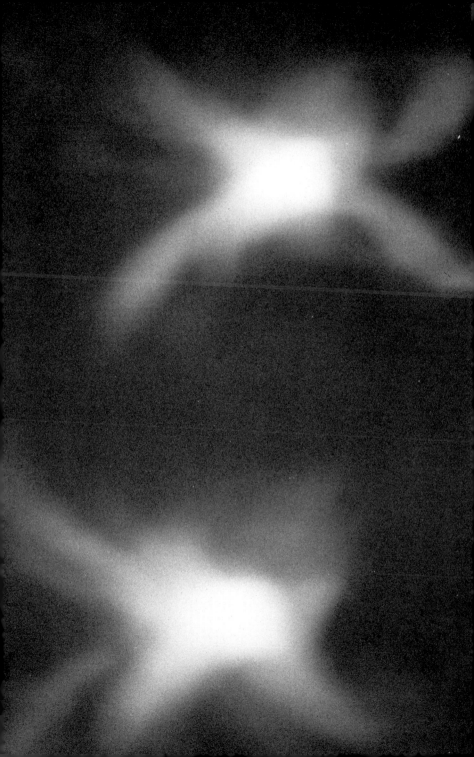

When Heaven's anger smites a man,
Who the cause shall truly scan?
                              —Lao Tzu

Without going outside his door, one under-stands [all that takes place] under the sky; without looking out from his window, one sees the Tao of Heaven. The farther that one goes out [from himself], the less he knows.

—Lao Tzu

Sincere words are not fine; fine words are not sincere. Those who are skilled [in the Tao] do not dispute about it; the disputatious are not skilled in it. Those who know the Tao are not extensively learned; the extensively learned do not know it.

—Lao Tzu

The Heaven-honored One says, "Sincerity is the first step towards the knowledge of the Tao; it is by silence that the knowledge is maintained; it is with gentleness that the Tao is employed. The employment of sincerity looks like stupidity; the employment of silence looks like difficulty of utterance; the employment of gentleness looks like want of ability. But having attained to this, you may forget all bodily form; you may forget your personality; you may forget that you are forgetting.

—Yu Shu Ching

For regulating the human [in our constitution] and rendering the [proper] service to the heavenly, there is nothing like moderation.

—Lao Tzu

These things in ancient times received
      the One:

The sky obtained it and was clarified;
the earth received it and was settled firm;
The spirits got it and were energized;
The valleys had it, filled to overflow;
All things, as they partook it came alive;
The nobles and the king imbibed the One
In order that the realm might upright be;
Such things were then accomplished by
      the One.

Without its clarity the sky might break;
Except it were set firm, the earth might shake;
Without their energy the gods would pass;
Unless kept full, the valleys might go dry;
Except for life, all things would pass away;
Unless the One did lift and hold them high,
The nobles and the king might trip and fall.

The humble folk support the mighty ones;
They are base on which the highest rest.
The nobles and the king speak of themselves
As "orphans," "desolate," and "needy ones."
Does this not indicate that they depend
Upon the lowly people for support?

Truly, a cart is more than the sum of its parts.

Better to rumble like rocks
Than to tinkle like jade.

                     —Lao Tzu

The Way is a void,
Used but never filled:
An abyss it is
Like an ancestor
From which all things come.

It blunts sharpness,
Resolves tangles;
It tempers light,
Subdues turmoil.

A deep pool it is,
Never to run dry!
Whose offspring it may be
I do not know;
It is like a preface to God.

—Lao Tzu

He who knows does not speak.
                    —Lao Tzu

Always without desire we must be found,
If its deep mystery we would sound;
But if desire always within us be,
Its outer fringe is all that we shall see.
                                        —Lao Tzu

The student learns by daily increment.
The Way is gained by daily loss,
Loss upon loss until
At last comes rest.

By letting go, it all gets done;
The world is won by those who let it go!
But when you try and try
The world is then beyond the winning.

—Lao Tzu

The violent and strong do not die their
natural death.

—Lao Tzu

My words are very easy to know and very easy to practice; but there is no one in the world who is able to know and able to practice them.

There is an originating and all-comprehending [principle] in my words and an authoritative law for the things [which I enforce]. It is because they do not know these that men do not know me.

They who know me are few, and I am on that account [the more] to be prized. It is thus that the sage wears [a poor garb of] hair cloth, while he carries his [signet of] jade in his bosom.

—Lao Tzu

The small man pursues after wealth; the superior man pursues after reputation. The way in which they change their feelings and alter their nature is different; but if they were to cast away what they do, and replace it with doing nothing, they would be the same. Hence it is said, "Do not be a small man; return and pursue after the heavenly in you. Do not be a superior man; follow the rule of the heavenly in you. Be it crooked, be it straight, view the thing in the light of Heaven as revealed in you. Look all round on every side of it, and as the time indicates, cease your endeavors. Be it right, be it wrong, hold fast the ring in yourself in which all conditions converge. Alone by yourself, carry out your idea; ponder over the right way. Do not turn your course; do not try to complete your righteousness. You will fail in what you do. Do not haste to be rich; do not follow after your perfection. If you do, you will lose the heavenly in you."

—Chuang Tzu

To be unthought of by the foot that wears it is the fitness of a shoe; to be unthought of by the waist is the fitness of a girdle. When one's wisdom does not think of the right or the wrong [of a question under discussion], that shows the suitability of the of the mind [for the question]; when one is conscious of no inward change, or outward attraction, that shows the mastery of affairs. He who perceives at once the fitness and never loses the sense of it has the fitness that forgets all about what is fitting.

—Chuang Tzu

To know and yet think we do not know is the highest [attainment]; not to know and yet think we do know is a disease.

—Lao Tzu

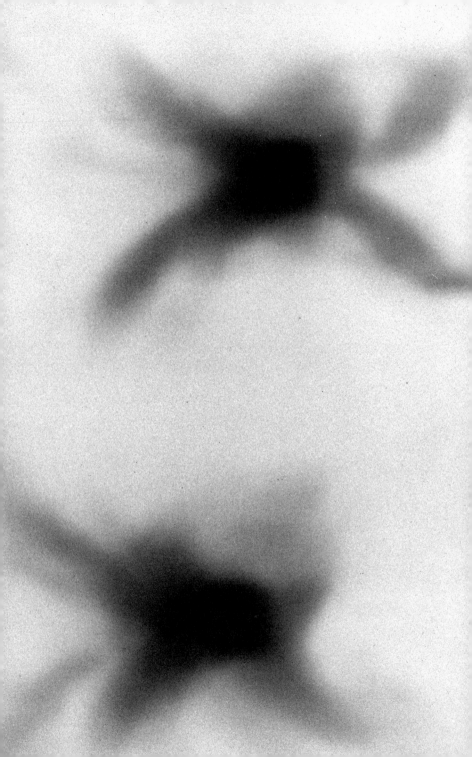

The Reason that can be reasoned is not the eternal Reason. The name that can be named is not the eternal Name. The Unnamable is of heaven and earth and beginning. The Namable becomes of the ten thousand things the mother.

—Lao Tzu

Everywhere it is obvious that if beauty makes a display of beauty, it is sheer ugliness. It is obvious that if goodness makes a display of goodness, it is sheer badness.

—Lao Tzu

Not boasting of one's worth forestalls people's envy.

Not prizing treasures difficult to obtain keeps people from committing theft.

Not contemplating what kindles desire keeps the heart unconfused.

—Lao Tzu

The dwelling of goodness is in low-liness. The heart of goodness is in commotion. When giving, goodness showeth benevolence. In words, goodness keepeth faith. In government, goodness standeth for order. In business, goodness exhibiteth ability. The movements of goodness keep time.

—Lao Tzu

Words that are strictly true seem to be paradoxical.

—Lao Tzu

Who can make the muddy water clear? Let it be still and it will gradually become clear. Who can secure the condition of rest? Let movement go on and the condition of rest will gradually arise.

—Lao Tzu